Courage for Daily Life

30 Day Devotional

Joyce Matanga

Copyright © 2023 by Joyce Matanga

All rights reserved.

No part of this book may be reproduced in any form or by any electronic or mechanical means, including information storage and retrieval systems, without written permission from the author, except for the use of brief quotations in a book review.

Scriptures taken from the Holy Bible, New International Version®, NIV®. Copyright © 1973, 1978, 1984, 2011 by Biblica, Inc.™ Used by permission of Zondervan. All rights reserved worldwide. www.zondervan.com The "NIV" and "New International Version" are trademarks registered in the United States Patent and Trademark Office by Biblica, Inc.™

Cover Design and Formatting by RLS Creativity https://qr.link/7lkNPU

All photos from Canva Pro Account

Paperback: 978-1-7390569-8-8

E-Book: 978-1-7390569-9-5

Contents

My Strength and Defence	1
Do Not Be Faint Hearted or Afraid	5
Be Strong and Courageous	9
Do Not Be Afraid	11
Nothing is Too Hard for You	15
I Have Overcome the World	19
Be Strong and Courageous	23
Power, Love, and Self-Discipline	27
Serve with the Strength God Provides	31
Examining Our Ways	35
Let Us Not Be Weary	39
I Will Fear No Evil	41
Finding Peace	43
When I am Afraid	45
Be Strong	49
God's Favour	53
Take Courage!	57
Courage to Speak	61
Having Faith	65
Sent	67
Set Your Minds on Things Above	71
Joseph Accepts Jesus as His Son	73
I Am the Handmaid of the Lord	77
Sanctify Them by Your Word	81

God Knows the Plan He Has for You	83
God Has Not Given Us the Spirit of Fear	85
Stand Firm in the Faith; Be Courageous	87
Trusting God	91
Being Confident	95
Take Refuge in God	99
Afterword	103
About the Author	105

My Strength and Defence
Day 1

"The Lord is my strength and my defence; he has become my salvation. He is my God, and I will praise him, my father's God, and I will exalt him."
Exodus 15:2 (NIV)

In this psalm we see David with the attitude of getting strength and defence from God. He is seeing God as his salvation and he is under compulsion to praise God as his father.

SELF APPLICATION - Be Strong and Courageous

What lesson can we learn from Exodus 15:2? I see that in life there are so many things we pass through but God can turn bitter waters sweet. When the Israelites murmured and grumbled,

Moses cried to the Lord. In life I have learnt to cry to the Lord. In life I have learnt to be strong and courageous.

PRAYER

Dear God,
You are my strength and my song: You give me victory on my life journey. Thank you that you are always faithful to your promises. Amen.

Do Not Be Faint Hearted or Afraid

Day 2

He shall say: Hear, Israel: Today you are going into battle against your enemies. Do not be fainthearted or afraid; do not panic or be terrified by them. For the Lord your God is the one who goes with you to fight for you against your enemies to give you victory."
Deuteronomy 20:3 – 4 (NIV)

SELF APPLICATION - Look to God

Where do we look for strength in our life journey as we pass through difficulties? This scripture teaches me to look to God when I face battles in life.

PRAYER

Dear Lord,

I ask you to give me the strength as I go through _____ . (Name what you are passing through.) Amen.

Be Strong and Courageous
Day 3

"Be strong and courageous. Do not be afraid or terrified because of them, for the Lord your God goes with you; he will never leave you nor forsake you."
Deuteronomy 31:6 (NIV)

SELF APPLICATION - Do Not Fear

Who are we afraid of on our journey of life? This can be at home, work community etc.

PRAYER

Dear Lord,
Help me to be strong and courageous in your word you have promised not to leave me or forsake me, help me to trust your word. Amen.

Inhale courage.
Exhale fear.

Do Not Be Afraid
Day 4

"Be strong and courageous. Do not be afraid; Be not be discouraged, for the Lord your God will be with you wherever you go."
Joshua 1:9 (NIV)

SELF APPLICATION - Be Strong and Courageous

Life can be full of challenges and tough decision, but even in the midst of challenges and hardships God counsels us to be strong and courageous. Are you currently going through hardships?

PRAYER

Dear God,
Help me to be strong and courageous and help

me not to be afraid for you have promised me to be with me wherever I may go. You are with me, you are in my house, family, work place, I can't thank you enough for your presence. Amen.

Take what you
NEED

HOPE   COURAGE   FREEDOM

Nothing is Too Hard for You
Day 5

"Ah, Sovereign Lord, you have made the heavens and the earth by your great power and out stretched arm. Nothing is too hard for you."
Jeremiah 32:17 (NIV)

SELF APPLICATION - God is with me in the hard times

Are you going through a very hard and complicated situation in life? I usually find myself in this. When I moved to Canada, I had a very complicated situation of being separated from my children and my husband for 7 years and this scripture encouraged me.

PRAYER

Oh Lord God,

It is you who has made the heavens and the earth by your great power and by your out stretched arm. Nothing is too hard for you, heal me and I shall be healed, save me and I shall be saved. Amen.

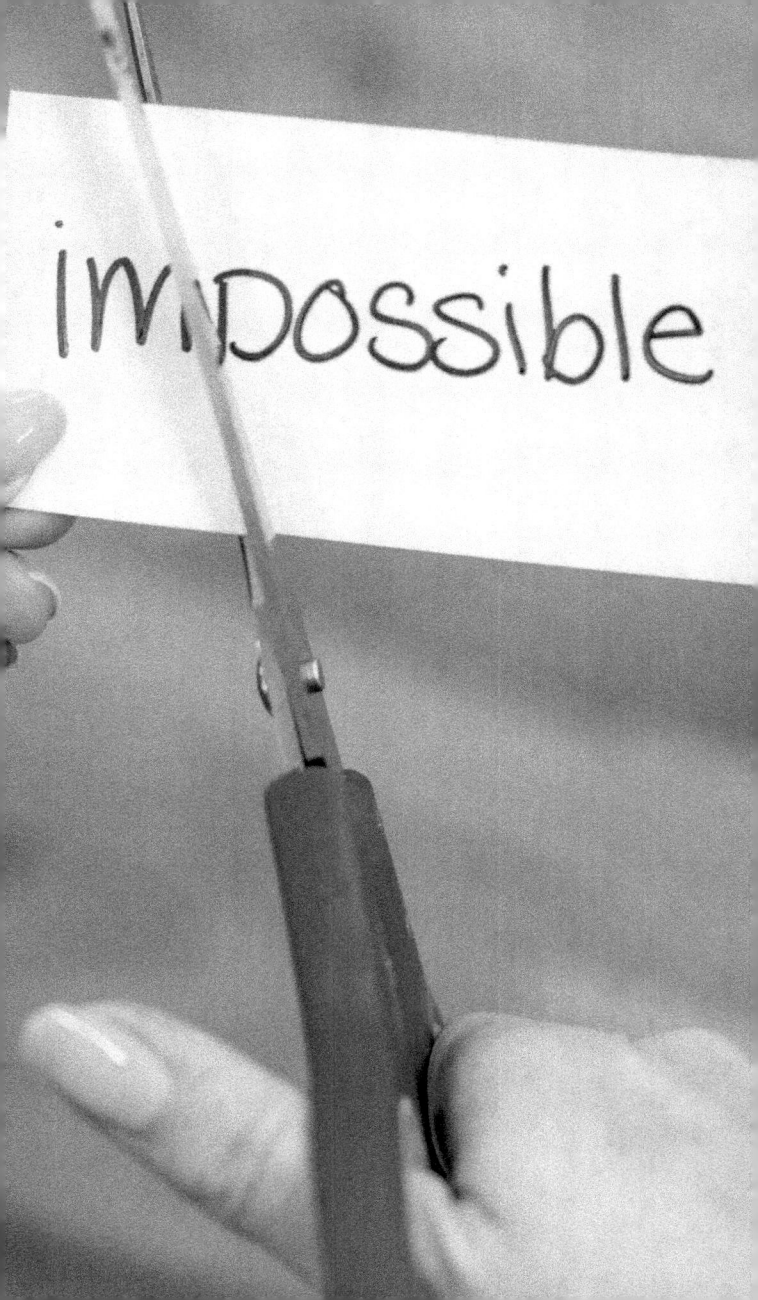

I Have Overcome the World
Day 6

"I have told you these things, so that in me you may have peace. In this world you will have trouble. But take heart! I have overcome the world."
John 16:33 (NIV)

SELF APPLICATION - Be of good cheer

Are you going through hardships, pain, discouragements? - Note, no human being on earth can escape hard times or tribulation because they are part of life. Following Jesus does not smooth life but Jesus reminds us that whatever we face or what comes we have to be of good cheer. Are you finding it difficult to be of good cheer?

PRAYER

Lord God,
I come before you, offering praise and songs for your works, Remind me of your victory on the cross of Calvary. Amen.
Remember to pray for others today going through hardships.

Be Strong and Courageous

Day 7

"Be on your guard; stand firm in the faith; be courageous; be strong. Do everything in love."
1 Corinthians 16:13-14 (NIV)

SELF APPLICATION - Be steadfast in faith

As Christians are we able to relate to what is happening in the world in relation to our faith? We can see a lot of dangers. Are we able to be steadfast in our faith and remain in the faith?

PRAYER

Eternal Father, all powerful, living and omnipresent,
I praise you with love and thanks for giving us

the Holy Spirit who is with us especially in the storms of life when courage fails us. Amen.

Power, Love, and Self-Discipline

Day 8

"For the Spirit of God gave us does not make us timid, but gives us power, love and self-discipline."
2 Timothy 1:7 (NIV)

SELF APPLICATION - Living our faith

When we look at 2 Timothy 1:7 we unpack the fruit of the Holy Spirit – Fearlessness, Power, Love and Self control.

Do we find ourselves falling short in using God's gifts? Do we remember to pray for those in leadership?

PRAYER

Dear Lord,

I pray that with the Holy Spirit who lives in me I can guard the minutes and hours you have given me to be self-disciplined and set some time aside to pray for those in leadership. Amen.

Serve with the Strength God Provides

Day 9

"If anyone speaks, they should do so as one who speaks the very words of God. If anyone serves, they should do so with the strength God provides, so that in all things God may be praised through Jesus Christ. To him be the glory and the power for ever and ever. Amen.
1 Peter 4:11 (NIV)

SELF APPLICATION - Clothing ourselves with humility

I have been asking myself this question in the last four months: Am I being humble as I relate to my sisters, workmates and many other people? The personal application here is to see if we are clothing ourselves with humility towards one another because God opposes the proud but shows favour to the humble. (James 4:6)

PRAYER

Dear Lord,
Turning to you in prayer is the last thing that crosses my mind as I move on through the journey of life. By the power of your Spirit inspire me to pray in all things. Not out of self-righteousness but as a sign of my dependence and trust in you. Amen.

Examining Our Ways
Day 10

"Let us examine our ways and test them, and let us return to the Lord." Lamentations 3:40 (NIV)

SELF APPLICATION - Testing our ways

Do we find it easy to examine our ways and test them according to the word of God?

Let us take a few minutes to examine our ways.

PRAYER

Dear God,
Thank you for the gift of life. Instead of complaining that things are bad, help me to have

courage and hope that things will be better. Amen.

Let Us Not Be Weary
Day 11

"Let us not become weary in doing good, for at the proper time we will reap a harvest if we do not give up."
Galatians 6:9 (NIV)

SELF APPLICATION

Do you find yourself getting weary in doing something for somebody, especially if the duration is long?

How do you view yourself in this passage?

<u>Summary</u>: Let us go out and do good to others.

PRAYER

Dear God,
Help me not to grow weary in doing good to others. Amen.

Kind
words
cost
nothing

I Will Fear No Evil
Day 12

"Even though I walk through the darkest valley, I will fear no evil for you are with me; your rod and your staff, they comfort me."
Psalm 23:4 (NIV)

SELF APPLICATION

We all face hard times in our lives, whether smaller or big. During this time it is hard to find strength and courage to put on a brave face.

Is there something you are facing where you need courage?

PRAYER

Dear God,
Sometimes life can be hard. Help me to find strength and courage in you. Amen.

Finding Peace
Day 13

"If you really know me, you will know my Father as well. From now on, you do not know him and have seen him." John 14:7 (NIV)

SELF APPLICATION

Knowing Jesus as a personal saviour is very important. Can we say we have known him and how have we known him. What can we say about the peace Jesus gives to the world?

PRAYER

Dear Lord,
You have taught me that you give peace and not as the world gives. Today, I pray for people going through trouble (Name them, for example, homeless people, widows etc.)

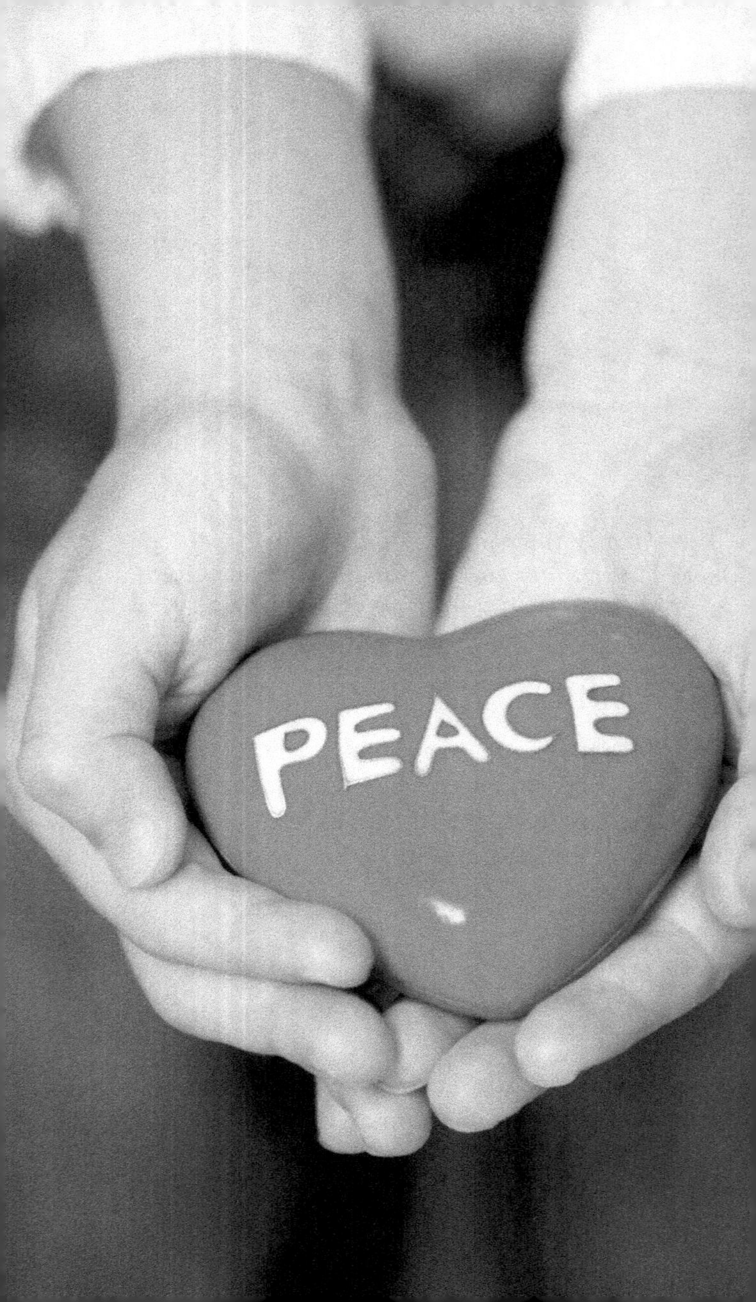
PEACE

When I am Afraid
Day 14

"When I am afraid, I put my trust in you. In God, whose word I praise – in God I trust and am not afraid. What can mere mortals do to me?
Psalm 56:3-4 (NIV)

SELF APPLICATION

In your trials in life when you are scared of what people will do to you, where do you go?

Psalms 56:3 – 4 is a good Psalm to recite in such moments.

PRAYER

God,
We praise you for your love, your power, your grace, your mercy and your word. We ask to fix

our eyes on you in all sorts of fear in this world. Amen.

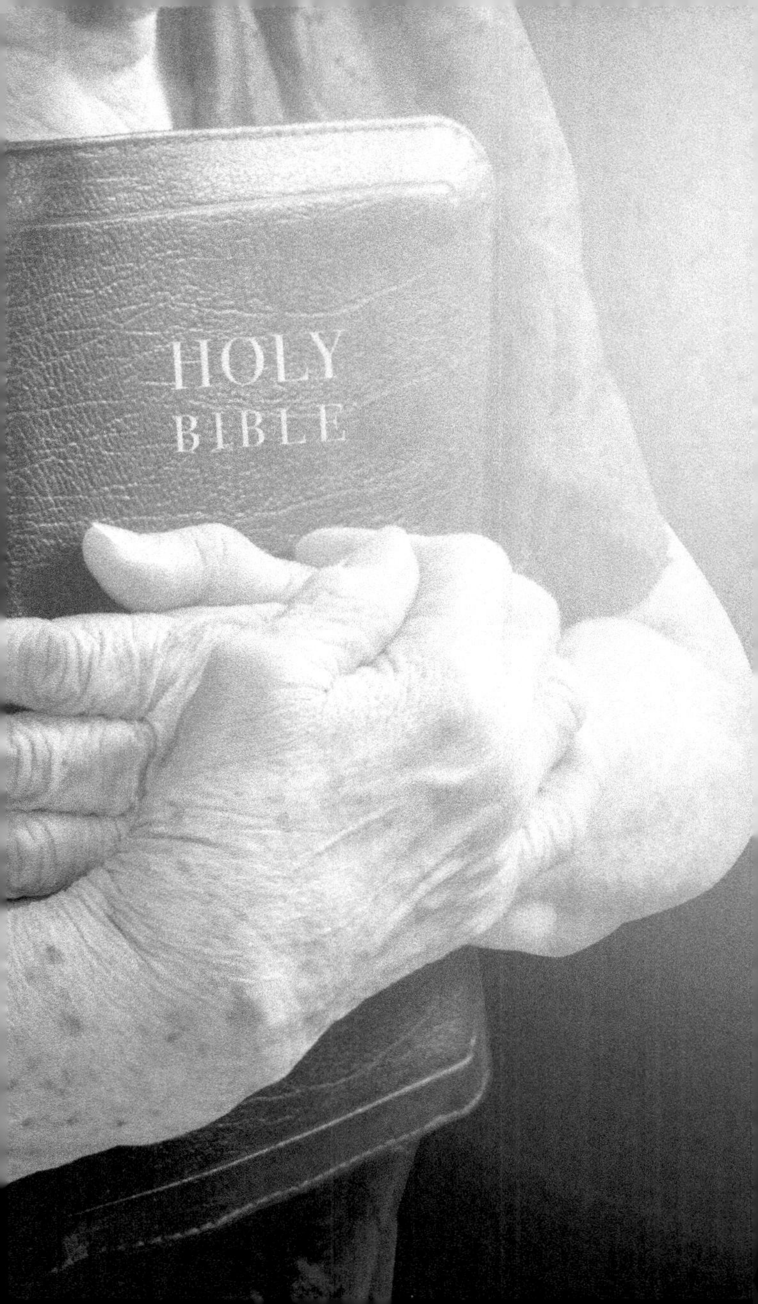
HOLY
BIBLE

Be Strong

Day 15

"Finally, be strong in the Lord and in his mighty power."
Ephesians 6:10 (NIV)

SELF APPLICATION

Who do we trust in the world of conflicts?
Where do we draw our strength from?

I have learnt in life that battles are there but we will win when we are empty of ourselves and allow God to fight our battles.

PRAYER

Dear Lord,
I pray that I will stand with you in truth around

my waist. I put on the breast plate of righteousness for your name's sake. Amen.

God's Favour

Day 16

"...and who has extended his good favour to me before the king and his advisers and all the king's powerful officials. Because the hand of the Lord my God was on me, I took courage and gathered leaders from Israel to go up with me."
Ezra 7:28 (NIV)

SELF APPLICATION

Ezra himself was a man of courage, yet he attributed his encouragement not to his own heart but to God. As individuals, do we find it easy to get encouragement from God's word when we need courage?

PRAYER

Dear God,

I ask that you show me favour in front of people and my work supervisors today. God, give me courage as I do my assigned tasks today. Amen.

Take Courage!

Day 17

But Jesus immediately said to them: "Take courage! It is I. Don't be afraid."
Mathew 14:27 (NIV)

SELF APPLICATION

The disciples got comfort from Jesus' words when he spoke to them: "Fear not!"

As Christians, we also find ourselves terrified, exhausted on the life journey. How can the scripture Mathew 14:27 be an encouragement to us?

PRAYER

Dear God,
Today make yourself clear. Make your pres-

ence known as I seek to serve you and move on in my faith. Amen.

Courage to Speak
Day 18

Before the spies lay down for the night, she went up on the roof and said to them, "I know that the Lord has given you this land and that a great fear of you has fallen on us, so that all who live in this country are melting in fear because of you. We have heard how the Lord dried up the water of the Red sea for you when you came out of Egypt, and what you did to Sihon and Og, the two kings of the Amorites east of the Jordan, whom you completely destroyed. When we heard of it, our hearts melted in fear and everyone's courage failed because of you, for the Lord your God is God in heaven above and on the earth below. Joshua 2:8 - 11 (NIV)

SELF APPLICATION

We see God as a God who cannot lie as his promises are unbreakable. The world might knock us down but God cannot let us down. How do we look at God in times when we are afraid or struggling? Write your reactions down.

PRAYER

Father God,
The word that goes from mouth will not return to you empty but will accomplish what you desire and achieve the purpose which you sent it. I ask you for strength based on your word as I journey in this word. Amen.

Having Faith
Day 19

By faith the prostitute Rahab, because she welcomed the spies, was not killed with those who were disobedient. Hebrews 11:31 (NIV)

SELF APPLICATION

Let us look at the prostitute, Rahab. What do we learn from her? In this world there are so many difficulties that we go through. How can we apply faith in God in these difficult circumstances?

PRAYER

Dear Lord,
I pray that I may live my life by faith and in a manner pleasing to you. Amen.

FEED YOUR FAITH

Sent

Day 20

Then Joshua son of Nun secretly sent two spies from Shittim "Go, look over the Land he said, "especially Jerico." So they went and entered the house of a prostitute named Rahab and stayed there. Joshua 2:11

SELF APPLICATION

Joshua the son of Num sent out two men from Acacia Grove to spy secretly. This kind of preparation shows faithfulness, not lack of faith.

How can we apply what we learn from this study to help us in our tasks?

PRAYER

Heavenly Father,

Thank you for many lessons we can learn from Joshua. I pray that let me have faith to carry out your perfect will for my life. Amen.

Set Your Minds on Things Above

Set your minds on things above, not on earthly things. Colossians 3:2 (NIV)

SELF APPLICATION

In the midst of life, where our focus so often is set on the day-to-day grind of life—our families, our careers, our businesses, our friends, our dreams, our goals and so on—it can be very hard to retrain our thoughts to the heavens and the one who created us. How can we have our minds stayed upon God?

PRAYER

Heavenly Father,
Help me to keep my eyes on Jesus and the glorious eternal inheritance that you have reserved for me. Amen.

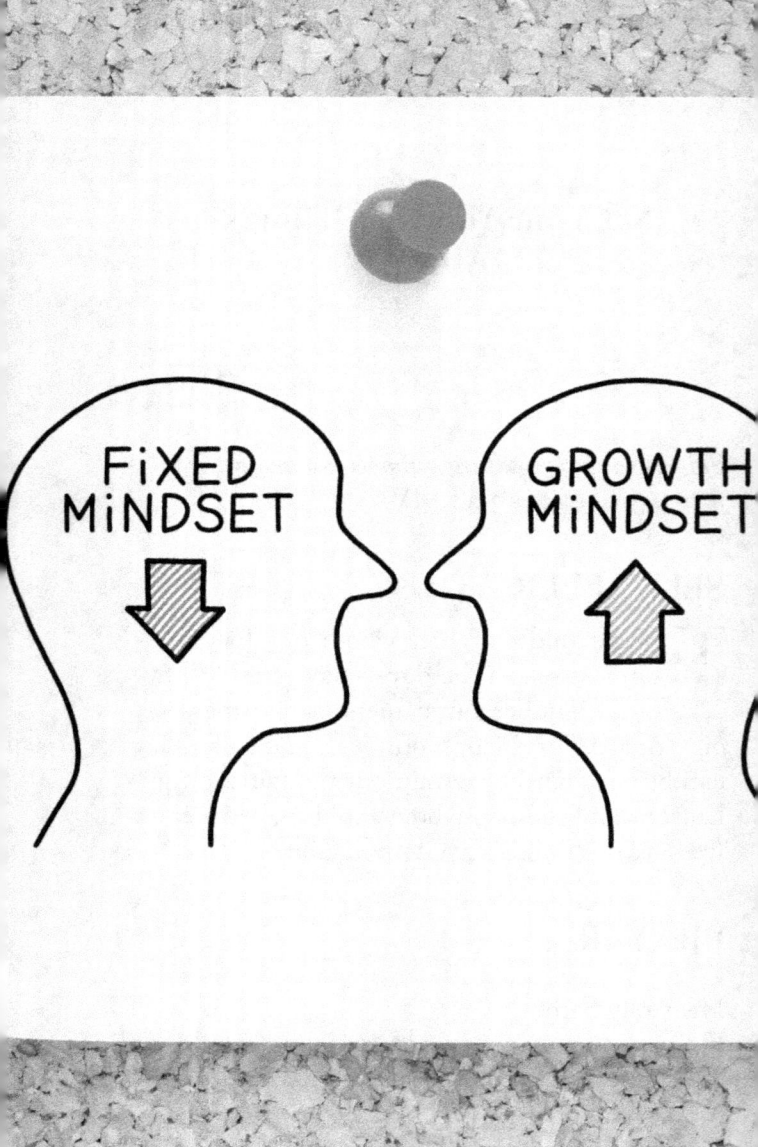

Joseph Accepts Jesus as His Son

Day 22

This is how the birth of Jesus the Messiah came about. His mother Mary was pledged to be married to Joseph but before they came together, she was found to be pregnant through the Holy Spirit. 19. Because Joseph her husband was faithful to the law, and yet did not want to expose her to public disgrace, he had in mind to divorce her quietly. Mathew 1:18 - 19 (NIV)

SELF APPLICATION

This is an interesting story about Joseph, Mary and the birth of Jesus. God interrupts Joseph's plans to divorce Mary.

How do you look at things in your life when your plans get interrupted?

PRAYER

Lord,
Forgive us for our sins and short comings. May you guide us through this day in everything we do. Teach us to be more loving, patient and compassionate to others. Show us how to accept your plans as we have learnt from Joseph and Mary. Amen.

I Am the Handmaid of the Lord

Day 23

"I am the Lord's servant." Mary answered."May your word to me be fulfilled."
Luke 1:38 (NIV)

SELF APPLICATION

Let us consider today that long before we were born, we were called by God to know Him, love Him, and serve Him. One of the hard things for Mary was to break the news that she was pregnant to Joseph and her parents.

Do we find it hard to break hard messages to loved ones?

PRAYER

Oh Lord God,

Creator of the universe and the Father who created me in the womb of my mother, I offer myself to you as a servant. Amen.

Sanctify Them by Your Word
Day 24

Sanctify them by the truth; your word is truth.
John 17:17 (NIV)

SELF APPLICATION

The only way to be justified is through believing in the Lord Jesus. How do you look at Jesus' suffering on the cross? John 17:17 gives us insights on Jesus' justification.

PRAYER

Oh God,
Give me a passion to know your truth and live it in both word and deed. May I reflect on your word. I pray in Jesus' name. Amen.

God Knows the Plan He Has for You

Day 25

"For I know the plans I have for you," declares the LORD, "plans to prosper you and not to harm you, plans to give you hope and a future."
Jeremiah 29:11 (NIV)

SELF APPLICATION

Many Christians find it difficult to see God's plan when they are in a difficult situation, but note that God is not a man. He cannot lie. Know that God loves you and has good plans for you.

PRAYER

Give me faith, O Lord, during the times I am weary, discouraged and beaten down. Inspire me to trust your promises.

God Has Not Given Us the Spirit of Fear

Day 26

For the Spirit God gave us does not make us timid, but gives us power, love and self-discipline.
2 Timothy 1:7 (NIV)

SELF APPLICATION

This world is full of challenges and uncertainty. What is 2 Timothy 1:7 reminding us? I see that God has given us the Spirit of boldness and not fear.

How do we apply sound mind where we meet challenging situations mentally?

PRAYER

Thank you Lord for keeping us stable and calm even in the midst of challenging situations. Amen.

Stand Firm in the Faith; Be Courageous

Day 27

Be on your guard; stand firm in the faith; be courageous; be strong.
1 Corinthians 16:13 (NIV)

SELF APPLICATION

As Christians we find ourselves facing things that are corrupting in the ways of the world. Do you find it hard to have courage to stand firm in your faith?

I find I meet people that try to corrupt or divide or change my faith. It is important to stand on the word of God.

PRAYER

Heavenly Father,
Thank you for another day of life. Help me to

be vigilant and to stand firm in my faith. I pray that you give me courage and strength to face whatever comes my way today in Jesus' name. Amen.

Trusting God
Day 28

Trust in the Lord with all your heart and lean not on your own understanding; in all your ways submit to him, and he will make your paths straight. Do not be wise in your own eyes; fear the Lord and shun evil. Proverbs 3:5-7 (NIV)

SELF APPLICATION

I find Proverbs chapter three, verses 5 to 7 helpful in my journey of life. Proverbs three is a proverb written by Solomon to his son, instructing the son to trust God.

Do we include God in everything we do? What wisdom insights can we draw from this scripture?

PRAYER

Dear God,
We ask you to lead, guide us in our faith, work, church and everything we do. Help us not to lean on our own understanding. In all our ways help us to acknowledge you, and you will make our paths straight. Amen.

Being Confident
Day 29

Though an army besiege me, my heart will not fear; though war break out against me, even then I will be confident. Psalm 27:3 (NIV)

SELF APPLICATION

As we conclude, let's make a list of things we are more likely to fear. I came up with the following but you can add on to the list:

1. Fear of change
2. Fear of failure
3. Fear of rejection
4. Fear of something bad happening

PRAYER

God,
You are my light and my salvation, you are my sufficient, you show me the best way to live and work, help me to know you and help me to overcome my fears. Amen.

Take Refuge in God
Day 30

The righteous will rejoice in the Lord and take refuge in Him; all the upright in heart will glory in him!
Psalm 64:10 NIV

SELF APPLICATION

I ask myself these questions, "Do I take refuge in God? In this corrupt world, am I upright before God?"

When I leave home and I am at work I usually ask myself, "Am I living an upright life among people who are not Christians?"

PRAYER

Dear Lord,
Hear me as I pray to you today, protect me

from the attacks of the enemy, protect me from those who plan evil on me. Lead me not into temptations, in Jesus name I pray, Amen.

Afterword

My prayer is as you have journeyed through this 30 days devotional, you have been strengthened and given courage to go on and fight battles in the name of the Lord Jesus Christ, knowing from scriptures He is always with you. Keep praying and moving forward.

Your Sister in Christ,
Joyce

About the Author

Joyce Matanga was born in Chililabombwe on the Copperbelt province of Zambia. She is the third born child in a family of ten. Joyce was born with an abnormality on her head which kept on growing as she grew.

This condition has taught Joyce a lot. She went through traditional healers until one day she came to know Jesus Christ as her personal saviour .

Joyce has a background of nursing , midwifery and counseling. Joyce left Zambia in 2011 to come and start her life in Canada.

It is during these years of being away from

home she started writing her own stories. God has really shown Himself as God in her life.

As Joyce was praying and talking to God she felt what she has been learning she can share in a devotional and let people be blessed.

Joyce has also joined the Inscribe Christian Writers Fellowship which she feels has really been beneficial as a new writer.

www.ingramcontent.com/pod-product-compliance
Lightning Source LLC
Chambersburg PA
CBHW071400080526
44587CB00017B/3145